Island of the Pelicans

A Photographic Essay of
the Island of Alcatraz
by
John D. Mercer

Introduction by Patricia Mercer

CREATIVE EYE PRESS
Sonoma, Ca.

© 1976 Creative Eye Press

Library of Congress # 75-39153
I.S.B.N. 0-916480-01-1

Special thanks to Walter Chappell for
his interest and enthusiasm.

Printed by The Country Printer, Occidental, Ca.

This book is dedicated to the men who lost their lives at the Attica State Prison massacre, September 13, 1971.

Some time before the advent of man, a small rock emerged in the middle of a beautiful bay near the center of California. When the Spanish discovered the Golden Gate and the San Francisco Bay, almost two centuries after Sir Francis Drake sailed up the west coast, that same small rock was covered with Pelicans, who found it to be a most suitable habitat. Thus, the Spanish named the island, Isla de los Alcatraces — Island of the Pelicans. It was so named in 1775. The Spanish were content to let the Pelicans continue to use the island and found it of no use to man. It was not until California became a part of the United States that the Island of the Pelicans became useful for man.

In 1850 an executive order reserved the island, now referred to simply as Alcatraz, for public use. Within three years, U. S. Army engineers were on the island and five years later could boast of having built the first lighthouse and U. S. fortification on the west coast. Alcatraz became a military fort and a convenient place to keep confederate conspirators. By 1860, Alcatraz was being used to imprison people. By 1868 it was officially designated a military prison and the Pelicans lost their home.

From 1868 until 1933, Alcatraz served the U. S. Army by acting as a fort and disciplinary prison. Alcatraz's military prisoners were not as colorful as her later federal prisoners, but they were diverse and came from everywhere. The prisoners included hostile Indians, confederate conspirators, offenders against Army regulations, Spanish, German and Puerto Rican refugees and conscientious objectors. These prisoners, like others who followed, spent a lot of time thinking about escape from Alcatraz. But during its 65 years as a military prison there were only 25 recorded escapes.

On June 19, 1933, Alcatraz was leased from the War Department by the Justice Department. The military vacated the prison and the Justice Department, under the direction of Attorney General Homer Cummings, began planning for a maximum security federal penitentiary. The 1930's had plunged America into an era of unprecedented street crime with gangland wars and their leaders making a mockery of law and order. The nation was gripped with fear. Just putting America's gangsters behind bars wasn't enough. Either they were *sprung* by their friends or they ran their rackets from within the the prison. So Alcatraz seemed to be the ideal *devil's island* for America and Attorney General Cummings set about to make it a reality.

By 1934, Alcatraz—later to become notorious as *The Rock*, was ready to receive its first federal prisoners. The island had changed quite a bit from its Army days. The main cell block had been kept, but was now equipped with tool-proof steel, four steel doors at the entrance, each independently operated, sky high guard towers, and barbed wire cat walks. There were tear-gas canisters in the ceiling of the cafeteria, metal detectors at all entrances and exits; and the best prison staff money could buy headed by James A. Johnston. With Johnston as warden during those beginning years at Alcatraz, there were minimum privileges. There were no visitors allowed the first three months you were there, and thereafter, only family with a special permit from the Attorney General's office, could visit once a month. There was a rule of silence that allowed no talking among the prisoners. There was no commissary and men went into solitary, known as *the hole*, for possessing anything that was not of general issue, such as a stick of gum or peppermint candy. There were no newspapers, movies or entertainment of any kind and recreation consisted of an hour in the yard on Saturday. All letters were edited and then typed on prison stationary by a guard, and then delivered to the prisoner.

There was never any pretense about the purpose of Alcatraz. It was a custodial institution with no intention of rehabilitating its inmates. Warden Johnston said, *...Generally these men have had opportunities in other prisons to reclaim themselves; but now their records make it necessary for the government to lay emphasis on their security.* This attitude continued throughout Alcatraz's 29 years as a federal penitentiary. Alcatraz's prisoners felt the effects of this attitude while confined there. They had no hope of rehabilitation and little hope for their future. Men were not released from Alcatraz directly. The best they could hope for was to return to another federal prison from which they could eventually be released.

Although Alcatraz basically remained a custodial institution, by the late fifties, things had improved some for the prisoners. They had religious services, movies, regular recreation, more industry and therefore more time out of their cells. Still however, out of the $7.50 a day Uncle Sam was spending per man, only 4¢ was going towards education. The government still felt men could not be rehabilitated, just locked up and Alcatraz was still the best lock-up the government had. Escape from Alcatraz was at best difficult to impossible. But escape thoughts never eluded the inmates. Many waking and sleeping hours were devoted to elaborate and not so elaborate escape plots.

The first escape was in 1937 and the last in 1962. Between those years there were 14 escape attempts involving 39 men. Seven were killed, six drowned, twenty-three were captured and three are still missing.

The missing three led an outright dramatic and complex escape that was not only successful in freeing the men involved, but was also successful in offering the final push to phase out Alcatraz as a federal prison. The escape in 1962, was master-minded by Frank Lee Morris, who hosted an IQ of 133, just short of genius. Morris and John and Clarence Anglin, with the help of time and decay, managed to escape Alcatraz in the middle of the night and give themselves a valuable eleven hour lead. Morris and the Anglin brothers used whatever tools were available to dig away the vent in their cells. By 1962, Alcatraz was well on its way to the decaying state it is in today. Because of the salt-water used by Army engineers to mix the original concrete and the continual exposure to salt air, the iron reinforcements were rusting, and the concrete was crumbling. It would have taken Morris and friends ten years to dig the 18" to 2' hole around their vents, had Alcatraz not been decaying. As it was, it took them about a year. There was one hour each night when the men were allowed to practice their musical instruments. It was only at this time that Morris and the Anglins worked on their digging. While the digging was in process, the men involved covered up the hole with a cardboard painting of the actual vent; which they had painted during their recreation time.

When the hole was ready, the men went into action. In their bunks they placed blankets and a dummy head made from wax and real hair which had been smuggled from the barber shop. They climbed out of their cells by squeezing through the vent opening into a utility alleyway which had a maze of pipes going to the roof. They climbed 30 feet up these pipes to the roof, pried a bar across an air conditioning exhaust and squeezed through a 12" ventilator opening onto the roof. From there they still had to get to the water's edge. Since the night watch did not report anyone missing, no alarms went off until roll call the next morning. So the convicts slipped past the guard towers and into the water. By the time the alarm was sounded, the men were either drowned and washed out to sea, or a good distance away from San Francisco. They were never located, nor were any bodies ever found. Alcatraz officials blamed the poor condition of the structures for the escape and pressures began to phase-out Alcatraz.

The phasing out of Alcatraz received little opposition and for the most part was publicly supported. From the very first, Alcatraz had to be padded with small fry, to bring it up to anything like penitentiary strength. There were never enough public enemies to fill the island to capacity. By 1961, two years before the phase-out was completed, Alcatraz housed only multiple car theives, forgers and burglers; who had run afoul of some federal law, but, who could just as well been housed in a dozen less expensive institutions. During the last decade, men were sent to Alcatraz because they were disliked by someone, they didn't co-operate, they were insolent or politically unpopular; or any other whimsical reason by the people in charge. By 1963, Alcatraz was mostly just expensive and unpopular. The structures were decaying and public enemies such as America saw in the Thirties were on the decline. The idea of a penitentiary without rehabilitation was socially unpopular and had been proven psychologically unhealthy. In 1963, Attorney General Robert Kennedy ordered Alcatraz closed. So ended the notorious keep-place for such infamous men as Al Capone, Machine Gun Kelly, Doc Barker, Robert (Birdman) Stroud, and 1,572 other less infamous men.

Alcatraz was abandoned. It was turned over to the Government Service Agency as surplus property and allowed to rest. Alcatraz rested in the middle of San Francisco Bay, bearing the burdensome structures that reminded it of man's influence. Bright yellow oxtails bloomed every spring; while during the other seasons, red ice plant mingled with evergreen bushes and eucalyptus trees. Alcatraz began to feel free again, but it was allowed to remain surplus property and free for only six short years.

In the fall of 1969, Alcatraz began its third journey into America's annals of history. Its period of freedom and rest was over. On November 8, 1969, the Indians landed on Alcatraz and claimed the island in the name of Indians of All Tribes. These native Americans wanted four things for Alcatraz: a center for native American studies, an Indian center for ecology, an American Indian spiritual center and an Indian training center. The Indians made their demands and settled onto the island, for what turned out to be 19 months of living under less than standard American conditions.

The Government Service Agency attended to negotiations with the Indian leaders. No agreements could be reached. The Indians demanded iron-clad agreements and the government wanted them off the island before they would make any agreements. Not wishing to remove their only lever, the

Indians stayed on the island. The government cut off the electricity to Alcatraz and stopped the delivery of fresh water. Still the Indians stayed. With the help of their friends on the mainland, food and water continued to be supplied.

As the weeks dragged on into months and the months to a second year, the strength of the Indian movement on Alcatraz began to weaken. Plagued by death, inner-tribal jealousies, lack of strong leadership and bad press; the Indians slowly left Alcatraz. On June 11, 1971, the last Indians were removed from the island. When the federal marshalls arrived to remove them, there were only 15 people left.

Although not especially successful at Alcatraz, the Indian movement did spread to other parts of the nation. Bureau of Indian Affairs offices across the nation were taken over by Indians who wanted to run their own affairs. Many tribes began demanding the return of reservation and original lands. Alcatraz was the beginning of public awareness of Indian rights and the kindling of an Indian Rights Movement in America.

Shortly after the Indians left Alcatraz, President Nixon designated the island a state park. The island became the property of the Golden Gate Recreation District and in October 1973, was opened to the public for guided tours. Today, Alcatraz receives thousands of visitors a day, who tour the prison island with well-informed guides.

Alcatraz's history has surely not been one of which it can be proud. Alcatraz did not willingly become a means of suppression. It was a victim of its surrounding waters. There has been some hope sparked that its future may be more meaningful than its past. Still the torments of that past, lie within the decaying structures that rest on its soil. Perhaps the hope of its future lies with the Indians or with the wildflowers that somehow manage to bloom again each spring.

15

17

19

"There are no bad men; there are only men who affect us badly . . ."

Benjamin DeCasseres, 1922

23

25

"The outlawed being may offend aesthetically, but he cannot offend morally; . . ."

Benjamin DeCasseres, 1922

29

*". . . The place (Alcatraz) is at its best in the spring
when flowers turn the island into a riot of color."*

Attorney General Homer S. Cummings, October, 1933

31

"Evil treads the same path as goodness, but it goes further . . . "
Benjamin DeCasseres, 1922

41

" *We came to Alcatraz with an idea. We would unite our people and show the world the Indian spirit would live forever. There was little hate or anger in our hearts, for the very thought of a lasting unity kept us whole and in harmony with life. From this island would grow a movement which must surely encompass the world. All men of this earth must hunger for peace and fellowship.*

The idea was born and spread across this land, not as a fire of anger, but as a warming glow . . . "

Peter Blue Cloud
Alcatraz Is Not an Island, 1974